Michelle Obama: A Biography

By: Alice Cruz

Michelle Obama came from a humble, working class upbringing to become one of the most powerful women in the world. She worked her way from Euclid Avenue in Chicago's South Shore to Princeton University, Harvard Law School, and finally to First Lady of the United States. She became the first African American First Lady in the history of the United States. Her rise to success helped inspire an entire generation, and her work ethic, intelligence, and humility helped cement and support American policy throughout the world. She successfully worked her way up from a working-class family that viewed takeout pizza as a treat, to being a student at Harvard Law School. She fearlessly changed careers when she realized that she did not enjoy working as an attorney, and became a sought after non-profit administrator. Although she disliked the idea of politics, she loyally and fiercely backed her husband's rise to power.

Humble Beginnings

Michelle LaVaughn Robinson was the only daughter of Fraser Robinson III and Marian Shields Robinson. She was born on January 17, 1964. Her father worked for the City of Chicago's water plant, and was the precinct captain for his Democratic precinct. Her mother was a secretary at Spiegel's department/catalogue store, who became a stay at home mother when her children were born, only reentering the workforce after Michelle graduated high school.

She had an older brother, Craig, who was born 21 months before her. Michelle and Craig both shared the living room, which was converted into their bedroom. The family shared a small, two-floor apartment. They lived on the second floor of their two-story home, renting the upstairs one-bedroom apartment from their aunt. The apartment was within walking distance of Michelle and Craig's elementary school. The family apartment was located in a working class, mostly African American, neighborhood. Michelle's mother taught both of her children to read by the age of four, and Michelle and Craig both skipped the second grade.

The family enjoyed playing board games, and always ate dinner together. The whole household attended religious services at the South Shore United Methodist Church. They also frequently visited extended family, and regularly vacationed in a cabin in White Cloud, Michigan. Michelle attended Bryn Mawr Elementary School, where she excelled academically. By sixth grade, she was enrolled in advanced classes, and was identified as a gifted student by her school.

While growing up, her father suffered from multiple sclerosis, which further motivated Michelle and Craig to do well in school and become successful. Michelle's mother tended to her sick aunt and ailing husband. Marian grew up in Chicago's south side, and her five siblings all lived within 15 miles of each other in Chicago. Marian later worked as an assistant in the trust department at a local Chicago bank, and carpooled with her sister, Grace, who was also Marian's coworker.

Michelle attended Chicago's first magnet high school, Whitney Young High School. Whitney Young was extremely selective, and only the most qualified students were granted admission. One of Michelle's peers was The Rev. Jessie Jackson's daughter, Santita. The school was located in Chicago's Near West Side, and the commute took an hour and a half each way. It was one of the first schools in Chicago for gifted students. Michelle earned all As, and never received a grade lower than an A-.

While in high school, Michelle took science classes at a local community college. She originally wanted to become a pediatrician, and focused her learning in the sciences. Eventually, she decided science was too boring, and changed her career goals.

She took Advanced Placement courses, and was a member of the National Honor Society. She also was elected treasurer of the student council, made the honor roll every semester, and graduated in 1981 as her class salutatorian. Michelle set her sights on attending Princeton University, but many of her teachers told her to lower her expectations. Michelle, when reflecting on how she reached her goal of attending Princeton, said, "I was willing to do whatever it took for me to go to college. Get this -- some of my teachers straight up told me that I was setting my sights too high. They told me I was never going to get into a school like Princeton. Nobody was going to take my hand and lead me to where I needed to go. Instead, it was going to be up to me to reach my goal. I would have to chart my own course."

Princeton was Michelle's "dream school," and she dedicated most of her time in high school to perfecting her resume and qualifications, engaging in extracurricular activities and leadership opportunities, excelling academically, and forging strong relationships with teachers and administrators.

Her brother recalls Michelle was always studying, from the time she came home from school until she went to bed. She also earned money by working as a babysitter, and saved up enough money to buy a Coach purse. Michelle's work ethic and dedication paid off when she received her acceptance letter from Princeton University. She soon joined her brother, who had enrolled in Princeton two years earlier as a basketball recruit, and pursued her Ivy League education.

College Years

When Michelle first arrived at Princeton, she was shocked at how wealthy many of her peers were. She noticed that many of her classmates were driving expensive, luxury vehicles. She recalls never knowing an adult who drove a BMW, yet several of her fellow students did. With so many of her classmates coming from significant wealth, and very few African American students, Michelle felt unwelcome and out of place.

Michelle entered Princeton in 1981 at the age of 17, and noted that Princeton was "infamous for being racially the most conservative of the Ivy League colleges." During her first semester, the mother of Michelle's roommate asked Princeton to move her daughter to a different dorm room, simply because Michelle was African American. Princeton rejected the request, but Michelle still encountered classmates who were unaware of how to properly interact with African Americans. She recalls multiple white female students asking to touch her hair.

In her freshman year, she received a C on her Greek Mythology midterm, the first time she had ever earned a C in her entire academic career. She also became heavily involved in the Third World Center, which was a student organization that sought to offer increased support to minority students, running a daycare center and offering tutoring. She majored in sociology, and minored in African American studies.

During her senior year, her Professor told her, "You're not the hottest thing I've seen coming out of the gate." The comment struck a chord with Michelle, who decided to make the Professor regret making the comment. She became his research assistant, working tirelessly, and he offered to write her a letter of recommendation for law school, proving to Michelle that she could achieve anything she wanted.

Michelle's senior thesis, entitled *"Princeton-Educated Blacks and the Black Community,"* examined how black

Princeton graduates changed their perspective on race during and after their time at Princeton. In her introduction, she wrote, ""I have found that at Princeton, no matter how liberal and open-minded some of my white professors and classmates try to be toward me, I sometimes feel like a visitor on campus; as if I really don't belong. Regardless of the circumstances under which I interact with whites at Princeton, it often seems as if, to them, I will always be black first and a student second."

The paper explored racial identity. It discussed how the attitudes of black Princeton alumni were perceived by their colleagues, peers, and fellow alums, and how they changed over time. The thesis reviewed how comfortable black alums were with interacting with both black and white individuals, how motivated black alums were in helping and becoming involved in black communities, how they felt about lower class black communities, if they felt an obligation to help those communities, and their views on race relations between blacks and whites.

She shared that, while at Princeton, she became more assimilated with her white classmates, and her overall goals changed. Many of her goals were similar, if not identical, to her white peers. She wanted to pursue a graduate degree, and obtain a high paying, corporate career. Although she entered Princeton feeling that she was obligated to help other minority students and black community members, she realized that her values had become more conservative.

In order to obtain data for her thesis, Michelle mailed questionnaires to over 400 black Princeton graduates. However, less than 90 responded. Her research concluded that blacks, throughout their time at Princeton and after graduation, identified less with black culture than before they enrolled.

In 1985, Michelle graduated *cum laude* from Princeton University with a Bachelor of Arts in Sociology, and a minor in African American studies. She decided to become an attorney, and applied to several law schools. Ultimately, Michelle decided to attend Harvard Law School, and moved to Boston in 1985.

Her time at Princeton helped her acknowledge that she could be exceptionally intelligent without sacrificing her "blackness," or her cultural identity. She recognized the difficulty of recognizing and celebrating her racial identity at a largely white, upper class Ivy League school. Some black students integrated with white students, to such a degree that they isolated themselves from other minorities. Conversely, some African American students only associated with other black students, and openly resented the white, elitist culture at Princeton.

Harvard Law School

Michelle participated in Moot Court during her first year, and although she didn't win the competition, she left a sizable impression. She was smart, hard-working, well prepared, and fearless. She never shied away from asking objectionable questions, and was noted for never getting lost in the theory of law. She maintained a pragmatic, bottom line approach, always asking if the policy or case decision solved the actual problem.

She joined the Black Law Students Association (BLSA), and preferred to avoid the spotlight. She helped organize events, and worked as an editor for the BlackLetter Journal, which was a law review that focused on African American Issues.

Harvard hosted a workshop entitled, "The Constitution and Race: A Critical Perspective," in 1987, to commemorate the 200th anniversary of the United States Constitution. Professor Derick Bell was featured as the keynote speaker, and workshops were led by Professor Charles Ogletree (Michelle's mentor) and Professor David Wilkins. The event focused on questioning why the Founding Father's allowed slavery, and banned women and blacks from voting.

Faculty and students began to openly criticize the hiring practices of Harvard and other institutions. The lack of minority faculty members created uproar, as well as the fact that there were 9 white students for every 1 black student at Harvard Law. Michelle wrote an essay for a BLSA memo, entitled, "Minority and Women Law Professors: A Comparison of Teaching Styles."

Her essay advocated for the benefits of having more minority Professors. She argued that a more diverse faculty could provide new perspectives and greater innovation, and that schools should place more value on qualities beyond the resume and intellectual prowess. Additionally, she preached that schools should encourage more interactive, hands on learning methods.

Michelle also volunteered at the Harvard Legal Aid Bureau, which provided free legal services to low income clients. On average, only 60 Harvard students volunteered at the Legal Aid Bureau annually, and students who did become involved with the organization were required to devote at least 20 hours per week to their cases.

Volunteers would help draft motions for a variety of legal

issues, including utility termination cases, evictions, divorces, custody disputes, and HUD issues. The Legal Aid was located in a small house on the outskirts of the Harvard campus, and Michelle would take public transit to meet with clients and opposing counsels throughout Boston. Michelle was the attorney of record in six cases. Three cases involved family law and two dealt with housing issues.

Michelle graduated from Harvard Law School with a Juris Doctor in 1988. When reflecting on her entrance into Harvard Law, Michelle would later state she regretted not taking time off after graduating from Princeton.

After Graduation

After graduating Harvard Law, Michelle took a position as an intellectual property attorney at Sidley Austin law firm in Chicago. Her first year's salary was more than twice her parents combined annual income, allowing her to have a very comfortable lifestyle. In 1989, she met her future husband, Barack Obama, who was a summer associate that Michelle was assigned to mentor. At first, Michelle was impressed with Barack, but attempted to set him up with some of her friends.

She thought he was very attractive, witty, and charming. After a month, Barack asked her out on a date. The two went to the Art Institute for lunch, and saw the movie "Do the Right Thing."

Michelle's family didn't think Barack would meet her standards, and thought they would break up within a month. Craig stated. "We gave it a month, tops. Not because there was anything wrong with him. He was smart, engaging, handsome, and tall, which is important for a five-foot-eleven woman, but we knew he was going to do something wrong, and then it was going to be too bad for him. She held everybody to the same standard as my father, which was very high."

Surprisingly, Michelle and Barack continued dating for several months, and Michelle asked Craig to challenge Barack to a game of basketball. Michelle's father and brother believed that a game of basketball was the perfect means to learn about someone's character and personality. After their game of one-on-one, Craig told Michelle that Barack had passed the test.

In March 1991, Michelle's father died at the age of 56 from complications related to multiple sclerosis. Michelle's father was diagnosed with multiple sclerosis when he was 30 years old. It was a devastating loss, given how close Michelle was with her father. Worsening matters, Michelle's best friend from college died the same year from cancer at the age of 25. Michelle was in the room when her friend passed, and the tragedies caused her to reevaluate her life.

For the first time, Michelle recognized and came to terms with her own mortality, and asked herself if her current job made her happy. She concluded that law did not bring her enjoyment, and, although she was an excellent attorney, she wanted to pursue other interests. In July 1991, she left Sidley Austin and pursued a career in the public sector.

Changing Careers

After leaving her position as an associate with Sidley Austin, Michelle served as an assistant to Chicago Mayor Richard Daley in 1991. Shortly after, she became the Assistant Commissioner of Planning and Development. Two years later, Michelle became the executive director for Public Allies' Chicago branch. The organization provided paid internships to young people, to encourage their pursuit of a career in public service. She held the position for four years, and set fundraising records that stood for over a decade.

Michelle left Public Allies in 1996 after being offered the position of Associate Dean of Student Services at the University of Chicago. While at the University of Chicago, Michelle created and opened the University's Community Service Center.

In 2002, Michelle left the University of Chicago. She became the Executive Director for Community Services at the University of Chicago Hospital, and was promoted to Vice

President for Community and External Affairs in 2005.

Additionally, Michelle served as a board member for Treehouse Foods Inc. and on the Board of Directors for the Chicago Council on Global Affairs. She was known for always being overprepared for meetings, and putting everything she had into her work.

Falling in Love

After dating Barack for several months, Michelle told family members that she was focused on her career above all else. Michelle was attracted to Barack's intelligence, talent, and character.

The couple continued dating for nearly three years. After Barack passed the bar exam, he and Michelle celebrated over dinner. Michelle began discussing their future, telling Barack that he had to start taking the relationship seriously. Before Barack could respond, the waiter came to the table to serve dessert. On Michelle's plate, there was an engagement ring. Barack got down on one knee and proposed.

Michelle said 'yes,' and the couple married on October 2, 1992. On July 4, 1998, their first daughter, Malia Ann Obama, was born. On July 10, 2001, the couples' second daughter, Natasha, was born.

Politics

Barack first considered running for office in 1996, and Michelle was hesitant to fully embrace the idea of her husband becoming a politician. Michelle valued normalcy in her family life, and feared that Barack transitioning to a political career would destroy the family's privacy.

She helped fundraise during Barack's 2000 campaign for the United States House of Representatives. Barack served in the Illinois House of

Representatives from 1997 until 2004. In 2004, Barack won a seat in the United States Senate.

Barack began traveling frequently from the family home in Chicago to Washington D.C, putting a strain on the Obamas' family life. Michelle was angry at Barack, because she wanted to focus on her career, not raising a family alone. In order to address the situation, Michelle enlisted her family to help babysit and raise her daughters.

When Barack approached Michelle about running for President of the United States, Michelle was fearful of how the campaign could negatively impact their daughters. Eventually, Michelle reached a compromise with Barack. Barack agreed to quit smoking, and Michelle gave him her blessing to run for President. In February 2007, Barack formally announced his candidacy for President.

Michelle decided to transition to part time work during the campaign, reducing her workload by nearly 80%. Michelle's mother watched their daughters, sometimes overnight, so Michelle and Barack could focus on the campaign and election.

Unlike previous campaigns, Michelle was heavily involved in Barack's Presidential run. She attended numerous events, and was present during many campaign rallies and speeches.

Michelle worked on softening her image after being publicly labeled an "angry black woman." She began wearing more casual clothes, and appeared on shows like *The View*. Michelle was criticized for her sarcasm throughout the campaign.

She gave a well-received speech at the 2008 Democratic National Convention, focusing on her patriotism, and aimed to portray her family as a living example of the American Dream.

When Barack won the election and became President of the United States, Michelle used her newly-appointed position as First Lady to continue advocating for change.

First Lady

While First Lady, Michelle pushed for equal pay initiatives, healthy eating programs, LGBT rights, and veteran issues. In celebration of the enactment of the Lilly Ledbetter Fair Pay Act of 2009, Michelle hosted a White House reception for feminists, equal rights, and women's rights activists.

She sought to visit every United States Cabinet level department in order to better understand the White House, and to get to know staff members better. She visited both the United States Department of Education and the United States Department of Housing and Urban Development, to garner support for economic stimulus bills. She also staunchly advocated for bills and policies that Barack supported.

In 2009, Michelle was awarded the Barbara Walter's Most Fascinating Person of the Year award. One of the issues Michelle most passionately supported was addressing veteran issues and homelessness. She was often brought to tears when she spoke with veterans about their service, and pushed to improve health care for veterans and eliminating veteran homelessness. She often met with servicemembers, veterans, and their families.

After a rough campaign, Michelle's public image was poor. During the campaign, she stated that her husband's campaign made her proud of the United States for the first time, and this statement damaged her public image. She worked adamantly to become more likable to the public, and by 2009, 63% of Americans viewed her favorably. Leading Democrats stated that her transformation turned her into a "superstar."

She visited soldiers and their civilian family members at Fort Bragg multiple times, and invited numerous military spouses and family members to events in Washington D.C. While visiting Fort Bragg, Michelle stopped by the Prager Child Development Center to read Dr. Seuss's "The Cat in the Hat," to several dozen preschoolers.

Michelle was shocked to learn that families of deployed servicemembers had to rely on food stamps and government benefits to make ends meet. She successfully advocated for a raise in military pay in 2010, leading to a 2.9% pay increase for soldiers.

Both Michelle and Barack were awarded the Jerald Washington Memorial Founders' Award by the National Coalition for Homeless Veterans in 2012 and 2015 for their work to combat veteran homelessness.

Michelle was more involved in Barack's 2012 re-election campaign, and was viewed more favorably than ever before. She was viewed more positively than Ann Romney, the wife of her husband's opposition.

Additionally, her demeanor was softer and more relatable than in previous elections. Barack easily won re-election.

In 2014, Michelle publicly fought for the return of 276 female students who were kidnapped in Nigeria by Boko Haram. The group eventually released the hostages.

Michelle created the "Let's Move" program to fight obesity, which is one of the leading causes of death in the United States. The program sought to help children eat healthier and combat childhood obesity. In 2010, Barack created the Task Force on Childhood Obesity to support programs promoting his wife's campaign. She started an organic garden at the White House, and the produce and honey produced from the garden was served at official White House events. The United States Department of Defense strongly supported Michelle's efforts, as the military was facing difficulties with an excessive number of obese recruits.

Other policy issues Michelle advocated for included LGBT rights. She voiced opposition to constitutional amendments banning gay marriage, supported expanding civil rights legislation to cover sexual orientation, and promoted legalizing gay marriage nationwide.

Michelle traveled extensively during her time as First Lady.

In 2009, Michelle famously, when visiting England, hugged Queen Elizabeth II at Buckingham Palace. The move created controversy domestically and abroad, as hugging the Queen violated tradition. Otherwise, the visit went well. Michelle completed her first trip abroad without her husband in 2010, when she visited Mexico and spoke with schoolchildren. She shared that everyone can succeed, and that with hard work and responsibility, anyone can overcome their struggles.

After the devastation caused by severe earthquakes that hit Haiti in 2010, Michelle personally visited the country to assess the damage, and to offer hope and inspiration to its people.

In June 2011, Michelle visited South Africa, and met with Graca Machel, the widow of Nelson Mandela, and a well-regarded humanitarian and women's rights activist. Michelle visited Cape Town, Johannesburg, and Botswana. She brought her daughters, mother, niece, and nephew along for her fourth trip to the African continent. During the trip, Michelle met with South African President Jacob Zuma and visited Robben Island, which is where Nelson Mandela served the majority of his prison sentence. Additionally, she toured the site of the 2010 World Cup, and went on a safari.

To help soften international relations with China, Michelle visited China in 2014 with her mother and her daughters. She met with China's first lady, and toured the Great Wall of China, the Terracotta Warriors Museum, and the Chengdu Panda Base.

During a visit to Saudi Arabia in 2015, to express condolences for the death of King Abdullah,

Michelle was widely criticized for refusing to wear a head scarf and leaving her face uncovered. Women in Saudi Arabi are required to wear head scarfs, and her wardrobe choice was lambasted. King Salman ignored Michelle when they met, only shaking hand with Barack as Michelle bowed her head and stood away from the meeting.

In November 2015, Michelle visited Qatar, and attended and spoke at the 2015 World Innovation Summit for Education, which was part of the "Let Girls Learn," initiative. She also toured several schools, advocating and encouraging greater access to education for girls and women. She met with female students, and pushed for women's education advancements.

She also visited Cuba and Argentina with Barack and her daughters.

In 2015, the Obamas decided to attend the 50th anniversary commemoration of the Walk on Selma. The Obama's famously participated in the walk across the Edmund Pettus Bridge, and used the anniversary to help support racial equality and recognize the country's troubled history with civil rights and racism. The event also showed how much the country had progressed, recognizing the discrimination that caused the march and demonstrating the importance of Barack becoming the first African American President.

In 2016, Michelle helped campaign for Hillary Clinton. She gave several speeches, including one at the Democratic National Convention, praising Hillary as the most qualified candidate. She strongly criticized Donald Trump, and vehemently attacked him publicly for the statements he made in 2005 involving lude comments directed at women.

Pop Culture

Michelle Obama was often compared to Jackie Kennedy, due to her excellent fashion sense. In 2007, she made Vanity Fair's "10 of the World's Best Dressed People," list. She frequently wears designer clothing, and her fashion choices were idolized by many Americans. In 2008, People magazine named her one of the best-dressed women, noting that her style was refined, tasteful, and confident.

Additionally, she was listed as the 58th most influential Harvard alum, and was considered an excellent role model, especially for young black women.

Her fashion choices included over 50 different designers, but she also created pieces from retailers like Target and J. Crew in to her everyday wardrobe. Some of her favorite designers include Michael Kors and Jason Wu, and she has a particular affinity for sleeveless dresses.

She was one of only two First Ladies to be featured on the cover of Vogue, and the only First Lady to be featured on the cover multiple times. In total, she graced the cover of Vogue three times. Better Homes and Gardens featured Michelle on their cover in August 2011, and she became the first women to ever appear on their cover. She was also the first First Lady to announce a winner at the Oscars, when she announced that Argo won Best Picture in 2013.

After the White House

Michelle continues to be heavily involved in American politics. She joined former First Ladies Laura Bush, Hillary Clinton, and Rosalynn Carter in criticizing President Donald Trump's child separation policy, which entails separating the families of detained illegal immigrants. She voiced concerns when the Trump administration sought to curtail requirements of healthy food for school children.

She additionally has advocated for improving access to education, especially for children.

Michelle and Barack signed a multi-year agreement with Netflix to produce content, including documentaries, scripted series, and features in 2018. She continues her College Signing Tradition, which features high school students announcing their post-graduation plans on stage. She attended the Pennsylvania Conference for Women and the Women's Foundation of

Colorado's 30th Anniversary event in Denver.

The Obama's remained in Washington D.C. after Barack's second term ended. Malia has enrolled at Harvard, and Sasha lives at home. Sasha designed her room, and has a two-room suite.

She devotes time to the Obama Foundation, a non-profit created by the couple in 2014. The Foundation offers scholarships to the University of Chicago's Harris School of Public Policy, and oversees the construction of Obama's Presidential Library.

Michelle has published a book entitled "Becoming," which will be released on November 13, 2018. She continues to attend events such as the AIA conference, and enjoys traveling with her family. They have vacationed in the Virgin Islands, Indonesia, and Italy.

The couple signed a joint book agreement with Penguin Random House in 2017, which included a $65 million advance. She joked that her first plan after leaving the White House included lots of sleep. They purchased an 8,200-square foot house in Washington D.C. shortly before leaving the White House, and

Michelle had full control over the purchase.

She voiced her concerns at the lack of support by women for Hillary Clinton, stating, "I'm concerned about us women, on how we think about ourselves and each other. What is going on in our heads where we let that (President Donald Trump's election) happen? So I do wonder what are young girls dreaming about, when the most qualified person running was a woman and look what we did instead. That said something about where we're at. If we as women are still suspicious about each other, if we still have this crazy bar for each other that we don't have for men – if we're not comfortable with the notion that we can have a woman for president, compared to what? We need to have that conversation."

Although she has received public support for a potential future Presidential run, Michelle has stated she wants to focus on developing young leaders, improve education, and help create a better future.

Legacy

Michelle went through a phenomenal transformation during her eight years as First

Lady. She worked tirelessly to create a more positive public image, and was so successful that the public, as a whole, wants her to run for office

She maintained her focus on ensuring her daughters had a normal upbringing, and made sure to devote considerable time to her family, despite her husband becoming the most influential man in the world. She famously stated that her role was "mother-in-chief."

She is noted for reaching out to the private sector, encouraging grocery stores to open in underserved areas, and shared how her education shaped her positively. Opening up about the importance of education in her life, and encouraging young people, especially girls, to embrace school helped motivate youth to take their studies seriously.

She gave numerous graduation speeches, and expressed how she was impacted by racial and gender discrimination, which helped give hope to others. As time progressed, she strengthened her oratory skills, and became a very effective speaker. She helped increase awareness on racial issues in the country, stating that she woke up in a house that was built by slaves.

Her work promoting healthy eating habits and fighting obesity have raised standards for school meals. She has slowly become more relatable, helping other women feel connected about the work-family balance. Her struggles to protect her family's privacy while utilizing her platform to advocate for reforms resonated with many Americans.

When describing Michelle's tenure as First Lady, Elle Kurpiewski, organizer for the Democratic Headquarters of the Desert, stated that "Mrs. Obama has shown the kind of stamina and kind of force of will that Eleanor Roosevelt and Mrs. Clinton had. There have been few first ladies who have made their mark like that, and I think I would put Michelle Obama in that category."

Sherry Bebitch Jeffe, Professor at the University of Southern California's Sol Price School of Public Policy shared that, "She is probably the most mediagenic first lady we have ever had, and that's very important in today's society and in today's politics." Jeffe praised Michelle's mastery of social media, and her ability to captivate a large audience.

She was able to help shape the Obama legacy by interacting with people on social media, and her use of Instagram and Snapchat helped promote a lively and fun personality. She was the first person to use the Twitter handle FLOTUS.

Overall, Michelle Obama's life and legacy helped demonstrate that women can be successful through hard work and commitment, and that no dream is beyond the possible.